out there, somewhere

AF624645

Nadia Uccello

BookLeaf Publishing

Presentation by *BookLeaf Publishing*

Web: www.bookleafpub.com

E-mail: info@bookleafpub.com

ISBN: 9789357212519

First edition 2023

for sern.

ACKNOWLEDGEMENT

thankyou to paulo, captain and friend, for supplying a constance, laughter and a safe place on the sea.

PREFACE

if you've been called to the sea you know it. i've met people who've never seen it, people who are terrified of fish, people who think you can swim under islands. people who have no desire. and i've envied them. that giant, roaring universe of agony and beauty never stops calling out to your bones.

kristina

a single light, and the galley
shut down like a sleeping crank
watches for my next move.
what, little girl?
don't you know who you are anymore?
did your heart fall out on the flight over?
the laundry stares while i count my bruises.
one, two, you fell in love.
i'm not tired
but there are other reasons to go to bed.
i flip the single light, and descend, and the crew
stairs
creak accusingly.
three, four, five...

outside, the tide stretches to its highest
yawns, and drops its shoulders
for 6am.

smiler's crewhouse

it's crazy how we travel
and get to know a place by its people noises
its cooked food smells
its bars and house facades and broken concrete
and taxi cabs and the way people treat their dogs
but stare at this mountain for two minutes
and you will remember how all this
never was
do you know this place by its mountain?
do you see in the morning how she breathes in
and out?
how the rain curls around her
drapes respectful sheets before her
in thick torrents
a fleeting privacy
from the scurrying creatures, going about
in false measurements of time
(how old is a mountain?
what time do you start work?)

airlie

it ain't every night you go to sleep spinning
not just in rum and whisky spirals
not just in apocalyptic conversations with the
chef
not just in hatred of the chief tyrants
but a noxious slather of all of the above
and most importantly, a boat, spinning on anchor
sundeck lights obnoxiously ablaze
turning navy water a dark azure
in spite of the night
to spite one star
one orange, simmering, angry star
saying there you are, i see you
awake and aware and alone
— well almost —
i know you
and i'll cross your porthole seven thousand times
this night
while you sleep
and curse
and smile in your whisky dreams

mansions

houses face the streets nowadays
shaped like half of a half pipe — the stony,
walled front, a tall blockade
then as you move through them, off the street,
past their forbidding faces
(if you're allowed)
they slope downwards —
the living room's high ceiling
the patio's dismissed rafters
the yard's unfettered vista
the pool, where you walk about under nothing
but the sky
(perhaps naked)
insulated by a fortress but exposed
in your own safe way.
perhaps one day
they will be built differently:
the pool at the front, lapping at the sidewalk
the front porch, where energy floats in off the
street and rests for a while
through doors to wide living rooms where all are
welcome
then at the back, a huge wall
to reflect our faces
and keep all the love in.

newport, or object impermanence

something about the wind in this town, this quaint, sleepy little corner of the northern wintering world, makes me want to stay for ever. my muscles first shivered and shocked themselves stiff at the rude below-freezing temperatures; now they stretch and swing and the cold stirs in my bones like it belongs there. it begs me to go outside into the shipyard and whirl around and around and push my face into the sharp north wind until tears drag icy trails across my temples. i cannot concentrate in the salon, the galley or the cabins because the portholes let me see outside where the weak sunshine or the heavy rolling clouds yell something about coming out to play, come and find it... what is it? i run to the engine room before i lose my job.

the town itself isn't much help either. aged shingles peer down in stained brown rows from prim victorian houses. pastel-painted french windows are framed by balding trees sprayed with orange bursts of dying leaves and i try not to skip from the store to the cafe and back, did i leave my wallet here? any excuse not to go home.

i feel it taking me. every day i could stare longer. small parts of me float away on the wind and i don't think they come back.

at the same time i can't help but feel those pieces flying away from you.
i see them eventually collecting somewhere, all joined up to make Me again, and i watch myself realise i haven't made it back to you, but to somewhere so far away that you feel like a ghost. like a strange dream you shake off in the morning with a cup of tea.

are premonitions carried on the wind?

to be snatched away from you is one thing, but You draining away in a slow drip — this is something else. a satellite phone call where your happy voice chatters down the line about a good day and my appetite vanishes. the soft shake of a crewmate's head when i tell them how soft you are, how honest, how perfect the evil checkmate is down there in sunny florida. little things that nudge me toward a truth: i don't know when i will see you again. and i don't know how to deal with that.

so i go outside and play in the strangely comfortable icy wind, or lose myself stomping my foul-weather boots in a puddle, or stalk the giant seagulls or try to learn the boats. spreaders, spinlocks, genoas, jibs.

the wind is the only thing i trust right now. it's cold and it's alive and it's here. and that's all i've got.

how yachting works

yes hello i am a billionaire
i own... [tech].
all of a sudden, i want my own yacht.
(i'm not sure from whence the desire came.
i'm quite creative with my whims.)

but i can't drive the fucking yacht.
i just own [tech]. (that's much harder work.)

so i pay a captain to drive it for me
to argentina or jamaica or alaska or barbados.

the captain seems to need other people
to throw lines onto the dock
and wash my boat (i suppose it IS quite big)
and scrub acid into the teak
and iron out stiletto holes with a wet cloth
and joke about how 'they're ALL actresses'
so i suppose i must pay deckhands.
at least they understand me.

what! — someone needs to be able to fix the
boat
when it breaks?

(boats are apparently broken all the fucking
time.
not mine. i object.)
so i pay an engineer.

now i realise — in the bahamas, i don't want to
pour my own drinks
least of all make my bed
clean my toilet
make wine lists plan dinner events order the
right anniversary flowers pick chest hairs from
the shower drain make my guests laugh scrub
shit out of my favourite white underwear.
gross.
so i pay a stewardess (the least.)

and what a tight-knit team i have created!
how bonded they are! how lucky!
i will take these funny little servants
everywhere.
they may have small cabins i suppose
and their own tiny (adorable!) crew mess
where they can talk about crew things
when they're not crew-ing
(those midday naps are the trick, i tell you
i can go all night after those. the servants should
try it sometime.)

though i'm not completely comfortable with it, i will pay
for their food, their toiletries, and their medical.
(unless they're american
then they can take their insurance rates and fuck off.)

my PA pitched me an idea —
when i am not on my boat having sex with russian prostitutes
or sunning my glorious niptucked body
or fucking crewmembers for sport
or showing my Art Friends what i bought at Art Basel
— why not make money with my yacht?

the captain can network in his spare time, and find me
people with ALMOST as much money as me
to rent my yacht and my entire crew for a week.
ha! i suppose
i'm as good a travel agent as any
— hang on
how many weeks in a year?
apart from fuelling my yacht and feeding the less-rich people
i keep the rest?
— the servants might even get tips! everybody wins!

more charters, more tips! ha!

when neither of these engagements are
underway aboard my vessel
(i've named it after myself)
i suppose i shall waste odd moments of my time
wondering what the little servants are doing
— growing fat and lazy on my expansive dime?
perhaps i'll terrorise them with phone calls
where i threaten to turn up
but have no intention of doing so.
it keeps them on their toes.

which reminds me — i must have that short
stewardess fired
i prefer tall women.

me deck, you stew

during the day we hold objects that divide us, a pen, a cloth, a hose, a tray, we wrap our digits around tools and move them about to achieve things, then at night we retire and hold onto nothing, not even ourselves, we are unable, and our hands lie flaccid and flat and limp, resting from hours of use — for what? for important things, we suppose; but now they rest, curl and uncurl as we dream, our minds victim to what may come, our hands unable to grip or use or manouvre or change even a thing about this state of sleep that now commands us. our hands rest. our mind has let them be, and now asks them only for tiny, twitchy reactions to the wild unknown of our dreams. fleshed beings that move about with such power during the day: poor, wealthy, spritely, gnarled, smug and humble, all reduced to the same predicament: innocent languour, ghostly vacancy, powerless repose.

question: who are you when you're asleep?

answer: you're everyone.

passage journal clippings

i am sitting by the helm's big leather-stitched wheel in borrowed foulies, hair stuck to my face, stray rays of weak sun in my eyes. as we sail south trails of newport cold seep out of my bones and float back to where they belong and it's almost as if we were never in that christmassy little pirate village. and the sea is forever. our boat, our feet, are grown from it. it pushes, we are pushed; it swells and hollows and we follow. we are gingerly riding a creature that does not care if we live or die and would not intervene for better or worse and there is something very freeing about that.

—

frenchy has gone to get lunch and left me alone with the sea. its dark blue atlantic body boils a brilliant turquoise in the rumbling water behind us, and off to starboard shimmers an oily silver in the soft sun. if there was a day i was going to spew it would be this one. we buck and heel as only a hundred-foot sailboat with no sail can. our bow throws itself completely underwater once per set and sends small salty tidal waves purling down the scuppers to mill about the drainholes like the last guests at a party, if italians built the exit doors. the swell is a southeasterly 2-3 metres and the fastest we've clocked is around 6 knots. i made it up into the fresh air of the cockpit just in time. no matter if i hadn't really, i had nothing in me to throw up.

—

tonight the respectful calm that exists between me and frenchy is interrupted by swirling clouds of trillions of neon-green plankton glowing frothily in our wake. i squeal down at the billowing sparkles and hang as close to the rail as i can in the rollicking swell. frenchy snorts at me 'careful, madamoiselle.' i love how he comes off like he couldn't give two shits if i got sucked over the side, it encourages my bratty behaviour. but he is entertained, if slightly disgusted in his french way.

—

frenchy and fabio are sick and the rest of us are nervous. they are confined to the port guest cabins with rashes and headaches and swollen glands and bloodshot eyes. we are only hours southeast of bermuda. the doctor on the sat phone didn't say to turn back but we have altered our destination to sint maarten for quarantine. the boys' watch hours are split between us, 3 on, 3 off, in pairs, conditions are too gnarly for solo shifts. there are three days of passage left. dan and i look at each other in the cockpit, incongruously backlit by a fantastic sunset. 'don't touch your face ok? and eat everything green that sophie gives you.' 'ok. we'll be fine.'

—

afternoon of day seven. two days ago we found the tradewinds and have been beam-on to a 3 metre swell and 30 knots of wind ever since. i don't know how i'm ever going to unlearn sitting sideways. the starboard capping rail is drowned again, we are sprayed with salt again. the spray feels almost solid. i am made of salt. we slide down the back of the same wave and look up at another fat, rippling blue giant higher than three of me stacked. i sigh and turn my face to the buttery glow of another north atlantic sunset. the orange orb is muted by a sheet of thin cloud. i picture valerie valetta with her mane of lustless curls, turning her wasted face to the west, staring at the floridian sun, feeling peace course through her. some of us have to strive for the peace in our lives, work hard to feel warm or content or feel nothing for a few moments. i would trade the prospect of all future north atlantic sunsets for a long kiss and a hand on my waist. i think for me the working-very-hard has just begun.

devil's rock

i am lounging on a bed in the bow of a tiny sailboat, reading and trying not to sweat, which will be fruitless until the sun is long down and the irritating christmas winds are finally coloured by the night after a long day of ruining everyone's charter plans to st barths. i am distracted every so often by another accent floating past the breezy hatch — the caution of a scraggly island cat has become companion to my apparent habit of being places i'm not supposed to be. in the back of my mind the absence of an entry stamp in my passport burns like a brand, but the voices vanish down the dock, and i try to relax again and wrestle this shit novel into submission while tiny waves slap against the hull. i'm hungry enough to trek the dusty road to the grocery store again soon. sardines on saltines with radish and lime. last run a woman stared me down as i moved to pass her near the salt fish aisle. she told me god wants me to come back. i want to know what the shit he's doing in sint maarten.

concourse b is always closed

atlanta layover. i'm in georgia
but i will never know what it looks like. i will
remember
a tuscan chicken flatbread
and a lonely mobile recharge station
(god bless america.)

i never get tired of this.
homeless as a naked snail.
boots with worn wooden soles clicking through
the corridors faster than yours
because i am high on the fluorescent lights
and the smart, quiet marketing
and the sterile, sexless ambience
because as apparently homeless as i am
i am silently
deeply
relieved to be here.
a place of mind-bending human transportation,
my shrine to liminality, to my life so far.
you are all going home.
i am already there.

chief

3am i am slouched by the sink decompressing
with a mouthful of beef jerky head cocked to the
side listening to the dryer the waves bumping
the hull and my thoughts. she emerges like a
sleepy possum and looks at me horrified what
are you doing? just calming down. she says oh
then takes water and leaves looking strange. i
wish she didn't hate me why people don't look
up escapes me people who work with their heads
to their tasks and never think why, what am i;
people who are distressed by any ripple of
malcontent energy bent out of shape by others
looking, touching their eyeballs at their desks,
asking why. people don't look up. look up.

maho

6am i sit quietly, and the grey sky rains quietly on the harried turquoise sea. i know the shooshing sound of blown caplets and heavy sprinkles are happening but it doesn't reach beyond the airtight door of the silent galley. cold green-blue light ices the tops of things i'll set the big wooden table with soon — trays of glasses, cereal bowls, cutlery — smooth and straight and curved angles gleam, i will never be a morning person like valerie, the galley clock ticks, the fridges whine. past the wavelets the beach and hardy salt-fed shrubs keep tapering off and reappearing as we spin on anchor in the wind and rain. fellow boats bow and bob. and small i sit, quiet, cold and quiet.

sunrise outside nassau

sometimes i think
being out there
would soothe everything away

look at it, so soft
a big wet hug, eyes closed
for a while, rise and fall, rise and fall

then undulate away
settle down through fathoms
to sleep ever with a smile
for the creatures deep and wild

home, for my first tattoo

the way i live
days flutter past and past
and take with them
protesting fragments of who i am
even while they know what they are
they flit away.
they go.
i am hoping
when i slip back into
the rhythms that hum through home
— wounded and steeled against sharing or
caring —
the veins of true love that support those rhythms
will pump around me, past me
brush up against me with pulses of real
and open me up like a flower
like i used to be.
until then,
a reminder.

one day when i've finished killing myself
i'll live the life i should have
when i wanted it

flying out of sydney

i will never tire of it
the pure mortality, and absence of,
smashed together in a terrifying streak of
breathless nobodiness
30,000 feet above all of you
all of me —
everything i've done
everything you've done to me —
the one realm i ever truly split from my ego
and rest.
in utter wonder.
at god, or not-god, at humans, at engineering, at
clouds, at space, at the frost around the
bleed-hole, at the curve where we would
suffocate, at the war-torn water border between
thunderous fury and silent, sleek sunshine,
at the mercy of four hands behind a tiny glass
bubble. i rest. i always have.

an earth sign; somehow, my happiest place
is in the sky.

i am ten minutes late.

guilt bats at the door while exhaustion holds it shut. i suck down the biggest lungful of vaporised nicotine i can manage without vomiting, throw the rest of the fancy free gin down my throat and take one last look in the mirror before i barrel out the door. oh. eyedrops. he comes in. do you know where the eyedrops are? no, he exits and reappears. leah does. great. one more thing she'll use against me when she heads up to the pilot house to gun for my job. i kind of dribble it into the corners of my eyeballs while looking the other way because i'm a wuss like that. squint again at the mirror. not much better, especially with errant creases bulldozed into the white polo by the temp third stewardess who's probably well drunk by now. switch my radio on, the captain is chewing out our useless deckie again, turn the fucking thing down i have to talk to guests for christ's sake, shove the sticky door open into the violent light of the crew mess which is a pigsty even though we cleaned it two hours ago. here we go. dinner service 674 of day 3056 on charter, or whatever it is —

14 knots

the fury with which water thunders out of these
jet engines is beastly, violent; i imagine tripping
on the swim platform and falling in, and which
piecees of my soft human body would be
pounded or peeled away in the milliseconds
before it struck the tender we tow in our wake.

photograph

shiver

scurry low up the swim platform

there's a good girl

france, or burnout

the magic doesn't ever seem to return fully
i think it's frightened of me now
frightened of what i do
the company i keep
the lies i tell
so i am grateful
that sometimes
it still shows itself

on the melting horizon a cloud gargoyle poises, its mouth reaching, ears curled back, overhanging forehead proud and fierce. i stare for an age because it's huge and perfect. the shades of the world invert and deepen. a squeak off to my portside repeats on the starboard as two tiny terns swoop around the boat, their little white bodies turning green then red as they dodge the hulls for the joy of it. and i have never seen a brighter moon over a sea. it pours liquid metal over everything and begs my eyes to drink, but they belong to the glowing panel of arrows and numbers and rules in front of me.

well they're not really rules are they. they're options. endless choices ranging from life to death. and in between; panic, yelling, wreckage, drowning, hatred, cold, desperation, grief. or; serenity, boredom, introspection, forgiveness, discovery, appreciation, sleep, another day. choices. i could find the nearest tanker and ram this tiny cat into it at full speed. crumple the bulkheads, jolt everyone awake before they drown, and drown with them. turn us into drifting citizens of the crushing, pressing blue underworld, who flow by each other with polite nods and empty eyes, strange growths trailing us in blatant denial of the memory that we once had lungs with air in them. i definitely could.

why fear that knowledge? what is so terrifying about our capability to choose chaos and death? we choose life every day. we choose to wake up in a world of people exactly like us, delving into ugly souls to sustain the torturing and murdering of each other, of the beautiful creatures all about us, of the lush air bubble that sustains us — what is more frightening than choosing to see that again and again? certainly not death. certainly not the absence of this osmosis of befouled energy into our skins and organs and out again, into the next body full of fear.

even on the sea with a purple wind salting my hair strand by strand and miles from land i am not to feel free of it. there, a cargo ship full of rust and racism pouring the evil offal we make into the swell. does the sea cringe? i think i feel it. my own ship seethes with furious egos. tinted truths hum as we pass each other in the corridors and gangways, and fade back to a rhythmic whine of bruised pride and nasty plans and smug cocoons of righteousness, thick as the ignorance they were spun from.

you see the sea is not really the sea.

the magic doesn't visit me anymore because it does not know where i am. if i wanted to escape every last tangle of the benevolent spirit realm where creatures urge and push and whisper to us, then i have done a very good job, a very clean and well-executed job of it. the sea is a land of the drifting unconscious, of smiling hollow frightening faces that can be angry in a second and ecstatic in the next, solemn and wasted and friendly and trustworthy and traitors, all empty, all dead. i am alone without magic and i am dying with them. i become them. i learn to lie and smile. and as wisps of my living, screaming, protesting soul tear off and float away i become less traceable to those who would put me back together. am i beautiful yet? unconscious, smiling, floating, outbursts of fury

and laughter and falsities flicking across my face
for the ghoulish liars i bury myself with, while
those tiny wisps of soul whirl about alone and
sob in the dark for what they were.

i could choose death.
i would be refreshed.

galley eggs

one day i will write a book
of the abundant insanity i saw at sea
the mischief, connections and near-deaths
soul destructions, salt-sprayed wildness

then i will write another, just for me
and it will brim with days like this
my inner savage quietened by small things
my mental chatter asleep in the sun
my found coral, my favourite t-shirt, my newest book
and 1.30 pm breakfasts of poached eggs
local sea salt
and papaya pepper tonic
engineer and first mate out of bunks just in time
just me, mikey, tyler
and the merciful clouds

some of you will understand

here is a wink and a sip of tea
until your next slice of serenity
comes to set you free

make america hate again

four years of obstinate trauma bursts
no — five
careening steadily to a fever pitch
a continental wave, the crescendo
of prickling skins, aware of their colour
their sex
their former sex —
no one is safe, not if you're vulnerable
soft in ways unalotted by him
— white, wealthy, wizened
a thousand of them, cresting, commanding,
breaking upon the shore
of us. a hundred. it wouldn't matter. the
word of one of them
against a crush of us.
— smile, and bow.
concede.
be grateful.
bite it.
bitch.
blood coming out of her —
if only you knew how much, all over you
so much blood. all over you.

we became so tired
that our ears went home
but our eyes stayed to keep watch
our souls withdrew and our fingers stopped
gripping each other, and we just held ourselves
what if it happens today
what if it all goes away
or what if it comes for us.
however you pray
— do it quietly —
but do it.

today
a skinny black girl in yellow
and a striking black woman in purple
lift the battered chin of a nation
once again given to an old white man
but this time
with the sting of what can be
fresh on its back
and the fervour of what needs to be
bright in its eyes.

pearces creek

the terrestrial poetry of where i grew up
permeates what fears have seized me over the years.
because this place
belongs to me.
these trees know who i am.
soul echoes of my little wood-sprite self
with grubby knees and knotty hair
flit between shadows
along forested hairpin roads
laze in fluttering grass on the greenest
cow-dotted hills.
sugar cane rattles with mosquito-bit memory
in the wake of friends' new cars on old roads.
i've seen some dreamy latitudes
but nothing bows deeper
than coming home to country that
remembers you
better than you remember yourself.

www.ingramcontent.com/pod-product-compliance
Lightning Source LLC
Chambersburg PA
CBHW051748130826
49812CB00033B/1050

9789357212519